The Story of a Special Day
Volume 81

March

21

80th day of the year
(81st in leap years)
285 days remaining
until the end of the year.

by Michael Dobson

**Timespinner
Press**

Table of Contents

March 21 Quotations 2

Event of the Day 3

March 21 Holidays and Celebrations 7

What Happened on March 21? 13

Who Was Born on March 21? 24

Who Died on March 21? 42

March: The Third Month 59

March Symbols 60

March Events 61

Easter Events 65

March Zodiac Signs 68

What Day of the Week is March 21? 71

Copyright, Credit, and Contact 73

Cover: Puppet show on the Champs-Élysées, photograph by Charlik, for World Puppetry Day, March 21.

Back Cover: The month of March, from the French Gothic illuminated manuscript *Les Très Riches Heures du duc de Berry.*

March 21 Quotations

"Among individuals, as among nations, respect for the rights of others is peace."

> — *Benito Juárez, born March 21, 1860*

"Music is the moonlight in the gloomy night of life."

> — *Jean Paul, born March 21, 1763*

"If I had all the money I've spent on drink — I'd spend it on drink."

> — *Vivian Stanshall, born March 21, 1943*

"I regard the people as a great being, inspired by a single idea. This is my problem. I strove to solve it in [*Boris Godunov*]."

> — *Modest Mussorgsky, born March 21, 1839*

"Profound study of nature is the most fertile source of mathematical discoveries."

> — *Joseph Fourier, born March 21, 1768*

Event of the Day

Natalicio de Benito Juárez

Benito Juárez

Benito Juarez

One of the five great *Fiestas Patrias* (patriotic holidays) of Mexico is the Natalicio de Benito Juárez, or Birthday of Benito Juárez, commemorating the birth of President Juárez on March 21, 1806. (It's officially celebrated on the third Monday of March.)

Benito Juárez came from humble origins. He was born in a small adobe home in the village of San Pablo Guelatao in the state of Oaxaca. The mountain range where the village was located is in the mountain range now named in honor of Juárez, the "Sierra Juárez." His parents died when he was three years old and his grandparents shortly thereafter. His family was of Zapotec origin, described by Juárez in later life as *indios de la raza primitiva del país*, or "Indians of the original race of the country." This made Benito Juárez the first — and so far only — Mexican president of pure-blooded indigenous origin.

Juárez began school at the age of 12, unable to read or write and speaking only his native Zapotec language. A Franciscan monk saw great intelligence and drive in the young boy, and helped him further his education. He became first a lawyer and then a judge, and at the age of 41 was governor of the state of Oaxaca. Clashing with the military dictatorship of

Antonio López de Santa Anna (of Alamo fame), he went into exile in 1853. While working in a cigar factory in New Orleans, he helped prepare the Plan of Ayutla, which helped overthrow Santa Anna and establish a new constitution.

The new provisional government of Mexico established a constitution providing for freedom of speech, conscience, press, and the abolition of slavery, and Juárez became head of the Supreme Court. His *Ley Juárez*, which restricted the powers of the Catholic Church, along with other reforms, antagonized conservative elements, and a civil war known as the Reform War broke out. Juárez became interim President of a government in exile, fleeing to Veracruz. Aid provided by U.S. President James Buchanan helped the Juárez government defend Veracruz and later recapture Mexico City in 1861.

This did not end the troubles of the new government. Juárez, now the elected president, had to deal with an invasion by Emperor Napoleon III of France, who wanted to establish a Second Mexican Empire under his rule. While Mexican forces won an initial battle on May 5, 1862 (celebrated as *Cinco de Mayo*), once again he was forced to flee Mexico City and set up a government in exile while the French put Emperor Maximilian I of Mexico on the throne.

While the U.S. was sympathetic to Juárez, the American Civil War was more pressing. There was little appetite in Congress to engage in more military action, although U.S. President Andrew Johnson reputedly had the Army "lose" weapons and supplies near the border.

The French began to withdraw, abandoning the government of Maximilian I, who was subsequently tried and executed by a military court. Juárez was re-elected President of Mexico two more times, implementing progressive reforms, equal rights for the indigenous people of Mexico, and separation of church and state. The era of his presidency is known as *La Reforma del Norte* (the Reform of the North), and it is in recognition for his achievements that March 21 commemorates him.

Benito Juárez's name graces a number of cities, towns, streets, and buildings, both in Mexico and in countries ranging from the U.S. to Argentina to India. The Italian dictator Benito Mussolini was even named for him. His famous statement, "Law has always been my shield and my sword," is engraved in many courts and tribunals in Mexico.

* * *

March 21 Holidays and Celebrations

Cover Story
World Puppetry Day (International)

While puppetry as an art form dates back to approximately 3,000 BCE, World Puppetry Day is of more recent origin.

At the 2000 annual conference of the Union Internationale de la Marionnette (UNIMA), Iranian puppeteer Dzhivada Zolfagariho made the proposal, and in 2002 the UNIMA International Council declared World Puppetry Day to be held each March 21.

UNIMA is an affiliate of the United Nations Educational, Scientific, and Cultural Organization (UNESCO), with major centers in Prague (where it was founded), the U.S. (founded by Jim Henson), and in many other countries.

"A Children's Puppet Show," (中文：宋人嬰戲圖), 12th century CE, by an unknown Chinese artist of the Song dynasty.

Harmony Day (Australia)

Harmony Day in Australia celebrates the cohesive and inclusive nature of Australia and promotes a tolerant and culturally diverse society. On Harmony Day, Australians are urged to wear orange clothing or an orange ribbon. Over 6,500 Harmony Day events took place throughout Australia in 2011, primarily in schools and by community groups.

Human Rights Day (South Africa)

Worldwide, Human Rights Day is celebrated on December 10, the anniversary of the U.N.'s adoption of the Universal Declaration of Human Rights. In South Africa, it is celebrated as a public holiday on March 21 instead, in remembrance of the Sharpeville massacre of March 21, 1960, in which South African police opened fire on a crowd of black protesters of apartheid, killing 69 people.

International Day for the Elimination of Racial Discrimination (United Nations)

March 21 was proclaimed International Day for the Elimination of Racial Discrimination by the United Nations in 1966, with the date chosen to commemorate the Sharpeville massacre.

Independence Day (Namibia)

Namibia celebrates its independence from South Africa on March 21, 1990, following the Namibian War of Independence.

Library Day (Bangladesh)

Library Day in Bangladesh celebrates the birth of noted librarian and intellectual Muhammad Siddiq Khan (মুহাম্মদ সিদ্দীক খান).

Mother's Day (Most Arab countries)

March 21, the first day of spring, marks Mother's Day in much of the Arab world, introduced by famed journalist and writer Mustafa Amin (مصطفى أمين), based on a story of a widowed mother who devoted her life to helping her son become a doctor. The son then married and left without showing any gratitude. Egyptian President Gamal Abdel Nasser (جمال عبد الناصر حسين) declared the first Mother's Day in Egypt on March 21, 1956, from which the custom spread to other Arab countries.

Nowrūz (نوروز) (Iran)

Nowrūz, "New Day," is the Iranian New Year. It is celebrated on March 21 in most years, but the date can vary by a day or so in either direction. More on Nowrūz can be found in the "**March Events**" section of this book.

Salii (Ancient Rome)

The Salii, or "leaping priests of Mars," made their annual procession around the city of Rome on March 21 each year. King Numa Pompilus established the priestly order somewhere between 715 and 673 BCE. It consisted of 12 young men of patrician origin who dressed as archaic warriors, carrying shields. One of the shields was supposed to have fallen from heaven during King Numa's reign, and the other 11 were designed to protect the identity of the sacred shield. According to the ritual, as long as the sacred shield was preserved, Rome would be the dominant people of the world.

Truant's Day (Poland)

In Poland on March 21, students frequently skip school to mark the first day of spring. Variations of the tradition (often known as International Ditch Day) are celebrated on different days in different countries — often with significant repercussions from school officials.

World Down Syndrome Day (International)

On World Down Syndrome Day, people with Down syndrome and those who live and work with them organize events to promote public awareness. The date of 3/21 refers to the triplication of the 21st chromosome, which causes Down syndrome.

World Poetry Day (International)

March 21 was chosen as World Poetry Day by UNESCO in 1999 to promote the reading, writing, publishing, and teaching of poetry. Previously, the event had been celebrated in October, most commonly on October 15, the birthday of the Roman poet Virgil, and is still celebrated in October or November in some countries.

Youth Day (Tunisia)

Many countries celebrate Youth Day to honor their nation's youth. In Tunisia, it is celebrated on March 21.

Festivities Related to the March Equinox (International)

The *equinox*, a time in the solar year when the length of the day and of the night are approximately equal, is the occasion of a great many celebrations and festivities around the world. Because the exact date of the equinox can occur as early as March 19 and as late as March 21, these events move their dates from year to year. They are covered in the "**March Events**" section of this book.

Christian Feast Days

March 21 is the feast day of Nicholas of Flüe, and is also the commemoration of Thomas Cranmer, Archbishop of Canterbury and Martyr. It is also the earliest day that Holy Saturday can fall, covered in the "**Easter Events**" section of this book.

What Happened on March 21?

The abbreviation "O.S." on some dates refers to the fact that the Russian Empire did not switch from the Julian to the Gregorian calendar at the same time as the rest of Europe, and therefore some figures have two dates for their birth or death.

People whose original names are not in the Western alphabet have their native names in the appropriate script shown in parenthesis.

1556 CE – Archbishop Thomas Cranmer is Burned at the Stake

When the Church of England broke from the Roman Catholic Church over King Henry VIII's divorce, Archbishop of Canterbury Thomas Cranmer became the leading clergyman of the newly independent church.

A supporter of "royal supremacy," the idea that the King was sovereign over the church in his own realm, Cranmer developed the new standards and ceremonies for the Church of England, most importantly the new *Book of Common Prayer*.

When the Roman Catholic Queen Mary I came to the throne, she had Cranmer put on trial for treason and heresy. He was burned at the stake as a martyr to Protestants on March 21, 1556.

Execution of Archbishop Thomas Cranmer

1788 CE – **Great New Orleans Fire**

The Great New Orleans Fire began early in the afternoon of Good Friday, 1788, in the French Quarter, and quickly spread throughout the city spurred by a strong wind. Of the 1,000 buildings in New Orleans at the time, over 850 were destroyed. The only two fire engines in New Orleans were burned up in the blaze.

The city was slowly rebuilt in Spanish style, because New Orleans was then a colony of Spain, and most French architecture vanished from the French Quarter.

1800 CE – **The Papier-mâché Tiara**

Pope Pius VI was forced into exile in 1798 when French troops under the command of Napoléon Bonaparte took Rome and the Vatican, destroying or stealing all the ancient papal tiaras. Pius VI died a year later, and his successor, Pope Pius VII, was crowned in Venice on March 21, 1800.

Unfortunately, there was no tiara for the coronation, so a temporary tiara was made out of papier-mâché, decorated with jewels from the collection of aristocratic ladies in the area.

Although the tiara was supposed to be for the single occasion, it continued to be used even after a new silver tiara was made in 1820, because it was lightweight and comfortable.

Five popes altogether wore the papier-mâché tiara, and rumor has it that a sixth pope, Pius IX, occasionally wore it during long ceremonies.

1801 CE – **Battle of Alexandria**

The Battle of Alexandria, sometimes known as the Battle of Canope, pitted the French against the British near Alexandria, Egypt. The French under Napoléon had invaded the Ottoman province of Egypt with the goal of establishing a French presence in the Middle East.

The British, who had their own interest in the region and who were strongly opposed to the French Revolution and its aftermath, confronted the French in a series of battles, culminating in a British victory near the ruins of Nicopolis on March 21, 1801. The British then laid siege to Alexandria, forcing the surrender of the French garrison about six months later.

Detail from *The Battle of Alexandria* by Phi lip James de Loutherbourgh

1804 CE – **Code Napoléon**

The first modern legal code to be adopted widely in Europe was the Napoleonic Code, adopted March 21, 1804. It established freedom of religion, a merit system for government jobs, and elimination of privileges based on birth. It replaced a patchwork of feudal laws with a clearly written and accessible single code.

The Code Napoléon formed the basis not only for French law, but also the legal structure in Italy, the Netherlands, Belgium, Spain, Portugal, part of Germany, Romania, Egypt, and several Persian Gulf Arab states (mixed with Islamic law). While most U.S. law has its roots in British common law, the Louisiana civil code contains elements of the Napoleonic Code, as it was once a French possession.

1857 CE – **Tokyo Earthquake**

One of the deadliest earthquakes in history hit Tokyo, Japan, on March 21, 1857, killing over 100,000 people.

1935 CE – **Persia Becomes Iran**

On March 21, 1935, Reza Shah Palavi (رضاشاه پهلوی;) formally asked the international community to refer to his country as Iran, a name the people of the country had used to describe themselves since the early Sassanid dynasty, which came to power in 224 CE.

"Iran" means "Land of the Aryans," describing the connection between the various tribes that made up the region, whereas "Persia" referred only to the tribe of Pārsa. The Iranian language Farsi was originally Parsi, the language of the Pārsa, but there is no "p" sound in Arabic.

1937 CE – **Ponce Massacre**

On Palm Sunday, March 21, 1937, members of the Puerto Rico Nationalist Party were marching in protest of the U.S. government's imprisonment of their party's leader. Although the marchers had obtained a permit, the U.S.-appointed governor ordered the permit to be cancelled and directed the police to stop the march "by all means necessary" — but did not notify the organizers.

As the demonstrators began a peaceful march, police began firing submachine guns and rifles at the crowd, killing 17 and wounding 235, including women and children. While the governor claimed that the demonstrators shot first, a later independent investigation concluded that the police attack was a massacre. While the governor was removed from office, no charges were ever filed against police.

1943 CE – **Attempt to Assassinate Adolf Hitler**

On March 21, 1943, German Army officer Rudolf von Gersdorff hid two bombs in his pockets and planned to throw his arms around Adolf Hitler, killing them both. Hitler, however, changed his schedule at the last minute. Von Gersdorff transferred back to the Eastern Front to evade suspicion, and became one of the few anti-Hitler plotters to survive the war.

1945 CE – **Operation Carthage**

A British bombing raid on Gestapo headquarters in Copenhagen, Denmark, went tragically wrong when a British fighter crashed into a nearby school. Thinking the burning school was the target, some bombers dropped their payloads on the school killing over 100 people. The Gestapo headquarters were also destroyed, disrupting their operations and allowing some of their prisoners to escape.

1943 CE – **First African-American in the NFL**

African-American running back Kenneth "Kingfish" Washington led the nation in total offense and was the first consensus All-American in the history of UCLA football.

Originally, NFL owners blocked his draft by the Chicago Bears, but when the Cleveland Rams moved to Los Angeles, they agreed as part of the move to integrate the team.

The new Los Angeles Rams signed Washington on March 21, 1946. He was subsequently elected to the College Football Hall of Fame.

1952 CE – **First Rock and Roll Concert**

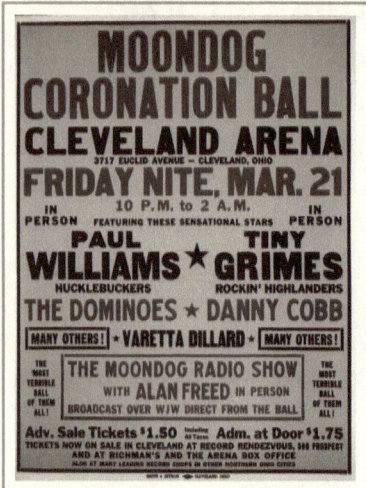

Cleveland disk jockey Alan Freed, credited with coining the name "rock and roll," organized the Moondog Coronation Ball, held at the Cleveland Arena on March 21, 1952. Acts included the Dominoes and Paul "Hucklebuck" Williams. More tickets were printed than there were seats in the arena, and fire authorities had to shut down the concert after the first song. It is generally considered to be the first major rock and roll concert.

1963 CE – **Alcatraz Closes**

The Federal prison on the island of Alcatraz officially opened on August 11, 1934. Designed for maximum security for the most dangerous prisoners, Alcatraz hosted Al Capone, Machine Gun Kelly, and Robert Franklin Stroud, known as the "Birdman of Alcatraz."

Alcatraz was much more expensive to operate than other Federal prisons, and salt water damage had caused erosion. At the order of Robert Kennedy, Alcatraz was closed on March 21, 1963, replaced by a new facility in Illinois.

1965 CE – **Launch of Ranger 9**

Ranger 9, designed to crash onto the lunar surface while transmitting high-resolution photographs, was launched on March 21, 1965, and crashed 64.5 hours later after successfully accomplishing its mission.

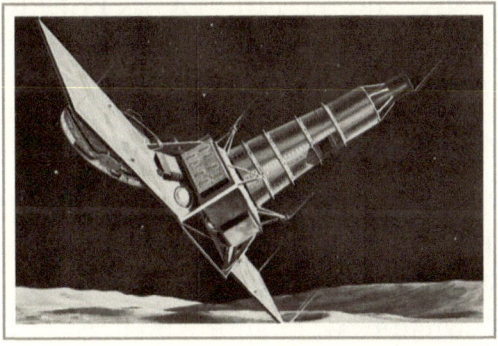

Ranger 9 about to impact on the Moon

1965 CE – **Third Selma to Montgomery March Begins**

On March 7, 1965, known as "Bloody Sunday," 600 civil rights marchers led by Martin Luther King, Jr., were attacked by Selma police armed with billy clubs and tear gas. Seventeen marchers were hospitalized.

A second march took place the following Tuesday, March 9. Prevented by a court order from conducting the full march, 2,500 protestors marched to the bridge where Bloody Sunday had taken place, and turned around. That night, three white ministers associated with the march were attacked and beaten; one was killed.

Finally, a judge ruled in favor of the march, and on March 21, 1965, nearly 8,000 people began the approximately 50-mile march from Selma to Montgomery, arriving two days later.

One marcher, Viola Liuzzo, was assassinated by the KKK, and the FBI's COINTELPRO program spread false rumors that she was a member of the Communist Party.

1968 CE – **Battle of Karameh**

The Battle of Karameh on March 21, 1968, pitted the Israeli Defense Force against combined Palestine Liberation Organization and Jordianian forces. Casualties were approximately 200 IDF, 350 PLO, and 320 Jordanians.

1980 CE – **Olympic Boycott Announced**

The 1980 Summer Olympics, were scheduled to be held in Moscow, the first time they had been staged in Eastern Europe. After the Soviet invasion of Afghanistan, U.S. President Jimmy Carter made an announcement on March 21, 1980 that the United States would boycott the Olympics schedule for later in the year.

In the end, 64 other countries joined the U.S., but some athletes from those countries competed under the Olympic flag rather than the flag of their own nation.

1999 CE – **First Balloon Circumnavigation**

On March 1, 1999, Bertrand Piccard and Brian Jones took off from Switzerland in the Breitling Orbiter 3 balloon, landing in Egypt on March 21 after traveling over 25,000 miles in the first circumnavigation of the globe by a balloon. Its gondola can be seen in the National Air and Space Museum.

Who Was Born on March 21?

Aviation and Space

Joe Sutter (March 21, 1921 —)

Boeing chief engineer Joe Sutter led the design team that built the Boeing 747.

Maurice Farman (March 21, 1877 — February 25, 1964)

Grand Prix automobile racer Maurice Farman founded Farman Aviation Works, which build over 200 types of military and civilian aircraft beginning in 1908.

Farman M.F. 11 biplane

George Owen Squier (March 21, 1865 — March 24, 1934)

American Major General George Owen Squier established the Aeronautical Division of the U.S. Signal Corps, the ancestor of today's U.S. Air Force. He also developed telephone carrier multiplexing, founded the Musak Corporation, and was the first military passenger on an airplane, flying with the Wright Brothers.

Alexander Mozhaysky (лександр Можайский) (March 21 [O.S. March 9], 1825 — April 1 [O.S. March 20], 1890)

Russian aviation pioneer Mozhaysky designed a pre-Wright Brothers airplane that Soviet sources claimed was the first powered flight. The Mozhaysky plane did get off the ground for a 100-foot hop, but only because it was sent down a ramp to gather lift.

Further research has shown that the weak engine and flat wings would have made actual powered flight impossible. Mozhaysky did, however, make significant contributions to flight controls and propulsion.

Business

Julio Gallo (March 21, 1910 — May 2, 1993)

Julio Gallo co-founded the E & J Gallo Winery with his brother Ernest. The Gallo Winery became the largest winery in America, controlling 25% of the American wine market.

Jim Thompson (March 21, 1906 — disappeared March 26, 1967)

American businessman Jim Thompson helped revitalize the Thai silk industry, becoming the most famous American living in Asia. He served in the OSS during World War II, working with the French Resistance. He went for a walk on March 26, 1967 in the Cameron Highlands, and never returned. He was later declared dead in absentia. His home, filled with extensive collections of Asian artifacts, is a prominent tourist attraction in Bangkok.

Forrest Mars, Sr. (March 21, 1904 — July 1, 1999)

Son of the founder of Mars, Inc., Forrest Mars invented M&Ms and the Mars Bar, and oversaw the launch of Uncle Ben's Converted Rice.

Film, Television, and Theater

Rachael MacFarlane (March 21, 1976 —)

Voice artist MacFarlane played the supreme leader in the animated series *Codename: Kids Next Door*, and in two series created by her brother Seth, *Family Guy* and *American Dad*.

Rhys Darby (March 21, 1974 —)

Darby played the band manager in the HBO and BBC series *Flight of the Conchords*.

Cenk Uygur (March 21, 1970 —)

Uygur co-founded and served as host of the Internet and radio talk show *The Young Turks*, and as a political commentator on MSNBC and Current TV.

Jaye Davidson (March 21, 1968 —)

Davidson is best known for the transgender role of "Dil" in 1992's *The Crying Game*, for which he received an Academy Award nomination.

Rosie O'Donnell (March 21, 1962 —)

Comedian and television personality Rosie O'Donnell hosted a successful daytime talk show and has been an activist for many causes.

Matthew Broderick (March 21, 1962 —)

Broderick was Bueller in *Ferris Bueller's Day Off*, and starred in *WarGames* and *Glory*.

Gary Oldman (March 21, 1958 —)

Oldman is best known as Sirius Black from the *Harry Potter* films and as Commissioner Gordon in the Christopher Nolan *Batman* trilogy. He was nominated for an Academy Award for Best Actor for his role in *Tinker, Taylor, Soldier, Spy*.

Sabrina Le Beauf (March 21, 1958 —)

Le Beauf played Sondra on the NBC sitcom *The Cosby Show*.

Brad Hall (March 21, 1958 —)

Hall was the news anchor on *Saturday Night Live* from 1982 to 1984. He married Julia Louis-Dreyfus, whom he met on the show.

Timothy Dalton (March 21, 1944 or 1946 —)

Dalton famously played James Bond in *The Living Daylights* and *License to Kill*, and Rhett Butler in the TV miniseries *Scarlett.*

Kathleen Widdoes (March 21, 1939 —)

Widdoes is best known for her role as Emma Snyder on *As the World Turns*.

Al Freeman, Jr. (March 21, 1934 — August 9, 2012)

Life member of the Actor's Studio, Freeman appeared in numerous plays, films, and TV shows, but is best known for playing Police Captain Ed Hall on the soap opera *One Life to Live*, for which he won an Emmy, and for playing Nation of Islam leader Elijah Muhammad in the Spike Lee film *Malcolm X.*

James Coco (March 21, 1930 — February 25, 1987)

Coco was nominated for a Golden Globe for *Man of La Mancha*, and for an Oscar and a Golden Globe for his performance in *Only When I Laugh*. He won an Emmy as a supporting actor on *St. Elsewhere*, and was Nick Milano on *Who's the Boss*.

Russ Meyer (March 21, 1922 — September 18, 2004)

Russ Meyer is known for his low-budget sexploitation films, beginning with 1959's *The Immoral Mr. Teas*, as well as such cult classics as *Faster, Pussycat! Kill! Kill!* and *Beyond the Valley of the Dolls*, with a script written by critic Roger Ebert.

Movie poster for Russ Meyer's *Faster, Pussycat! Kill! Kill!*

Jonathan Hale (March 21, 1891 — February 28, 1966)

Hale played Dagwood Bumstead's boss in the *Blondie* film series, Inspector Farnack in *The Saint* films from RKO, and appeared in the TV series *The Cisco Kid* and *The Adventures of Superman.*

"Broncho Billy" Anderson (March 21, 1880 — January 20, 1971)

Anderson was the first Western star in the movies, acting in over 300 silent films. He received the honor of a postage stamp in 1998 and is in the Western Performers Hall of Fame.

Literature and Journalism

Jonah Goldberg (March 21, 1969 —)

Conservative columnist Goldberg authored 2008's *Liberal Fascism*, a #1 New York *Times* bestseller.

Nizar Qabbani (نزار توفيق قباني) (March 21, 1923 — April 30, 1998)

Syrian diplomat and poet Nizar Qabbani is considered one of the most important contemporary poets in the Arab world.

Phyllis McGinley (March 21, 1905 — February 22, 1978)

Pulitzer Prize winning author Phyllis McGinley was known for her children's books and light verse. Her well-known works include "The Year Without a Santa Claus," *The Plain Princess*, and the poetry collection *Times Three*.

Jean Paul (March 21, 1763 — November 14, 1825)

German author Jean Paul was part of the Romantic movement, and is best known for his humorous novels. His works inspired several compositions by Robert Schumann.

Music and Dance

Kevin Federline (March 21, 1978)

Dancer and model Federline is best known for his two-year marriage to Britney Spears.

Eddie Money (March 21, 1949 —)

Rocker Eddie Money had hits with "Baby Hold On," "Two Tickets to Paradise," and Walk on Water."

Vivian Stanshall (March 21, 1943 — March 5, 1995)

Shanshall was a founding member of the Bonzo Dog Doo-Dah Band, from the proto-Monty Python BBC series *Do Not Adjust Your Set.*

Solomon Burke (March 21, 1940 — October 10, 2010)

Known as the "Bishop of Soul," Solomon Burke's hits include "Cry to Me," "Got to Get You Off My Mind, and "Everybody Needs Somebody to Love." He was inducted into the Rock and Roll Hall of Fame in 2001.

Son House (March 21, 1902 (?) — October 19, 1988)

Blues singer and guitarist Eddie James "Son" House, Jr., was a formative influence on Robert Johnson and Muddy Waters.

Bascom Lamar Lunsford (March 21, 1882 — September 4, 1973)

Known as the "Minstrel of the Appalachians," folklorist Lunsford's recordings are part of the Archive of American Folk Song. His original recording of "Good Old Mountain Dew" was the first commercial theme for the soft drink..

Modest Mussorgsky (Модéст Мýсоргский) (March 21 [O.S. March 9], 1881 — March 28 [O.S. March 16], 1881)

Mussorgsky is one of the best known Russian composers of the romantic period. Among his well known works are the opera *Boris Godunov*, the tone poem *Night on Bald Mountain*, and the piano suite *Pictures at an Exhibition*.

Modest Mussorgsky by Ilya Repin

Stefano Benedetto Pallavicino (March 21, 1672 — April 16, 1742)

Son of composer Carlo Pallavicino, Stefano wrote some twenty opera librettos, including Giovanni Ristori's *Calandro*, the first opera ever performed in Russia.

Public Service

Muhammad Siddiq Khan (মুহাম্মদ সিদ্দীক খান) (March 21, 1910 — August 13, 1978)

M. S. Khan established the information science and library management program at Dhaka University, receiving numerous awards for his scholarship. He received the Independence Day Award, Bangladesh's highest civilian honor, and his birthday of March 21 has been designated Library Day in Bangladesh.

John D. Rockefeller III (March 21, 1906 — July 10, 1978)

Third-generation member of the Rockefeller family, John D. III focused on philanthropic activities, establishing the Commission on Private Philanthropy and Public Needs and the Asia Society. He managed all Rockefeller programs with a social or charitable focus.

Nathaniel Woodard (March 21, 1811 — April 23, 1891)

Rev. Woodard founded eleven English schools to educate middle class youth, which are still operated through his charity, the Woodard Corporation.

Politics

Michael Heseltine (March 21, 1933 —)

British conservative politician Heseltine challenged Margaret Thatcher for party leadership, triggering Thatcher's eventual resignation.

Francis Lewis (March 21, 1713 — December 31, 1802)

New York representative Francis Lewis was a signer of the Declaration of Independence. His home was destroyed in the American Revolution, and his wife was arrested and kept for weeks without a change of clothes or adequate food. His son, Morgan Lewis, became governor of New York.

Religion

Shri Mataji Nirmala Devi (March 21, 1923— February 23, 2011)

Nirmala Srivastava founded the religious movement Shaja Yoga, and declared herself to be the incarnation of the Adi Shakti (Holy Spirit), as well as the Maitreya (future Buddha of the world) and the Mahdi (the prophesied redeemer of Islam).

Saint Angela De Merici (March 21, 1474 — January 27, 1540)

Italian religious leader Angela De Merici founded the Order of Ursulines. She was canonized in 1807. Her feast day of January 27 is the day of her death.

Saint Nicholas of Flüe (March 21, 1417 — March 21, 1487)

Patron saint of Switzerland, Nicholas of Flüe had a mystical vision of a lily being eaten by a horse, and thus became a hermit. For 19 years he ate no food other than the Eucharist. Visitors from all over Europe came to hear his wisdom His Catholic feast day of March 21 is both the day of his birth and his death. In Switzerland and Germany, his feast day is September 25.

St. Nicholas of Flüe (also called "Brother Klaus")

Science and Mathematics

Walter Gilbert (March 21, 1932 —)

Walter Gilbert shared the 1980 Nobel Prize in Chemistry for his work in DNA sequencing.

Joseph Fourier (March 21, 1768 — May 16, 1830)

Mathematician and physicist Jean Baptiste Joseph Fourier is known for the Fourier series, the Fourier transform, and Fourier's Law of Conduction. He was governor of Lower Egypt under Napoléon, played a role in the translation of the Rosetta Stone, and discovered the greenhouse effect.

Sports

Karolína and Kristýna Plíšková (March 21, 1992 —)

Czech tennis twin Karolína Plíšková won the 2010 Australian Open — Girls' Singles, and her sister Kristýna Plíšková won the 2010 Wimbledon Championships — Girls' Singles.

Adrian Peterson (March 21, 1985 —)

Minnesota Vikings running back Adrian "Purple Jesus" Peterson was named NFL Offensive Rookie of the Year in his first pro season, setting an NFL record for most rushing yards in a single game.

Marit Bjørgen (March 21, 1980 —)

Norwegian cross-country skier Bjørgen was the most successful athlete at the 2010 Winter Olympics, winning five medals (three gold).

Tom Flores (March 21, 1937 —)

Flores is one of only two people in NFL history to win championships as a player, an assistant coach, and a head coach, and was the first minority head coach in NFL history to win a Super Bowl.

Maurice Catarcio (March 21, 1929 — May 12, 2005)

Professional wrestler Maurice "The Matador" Catarcio is listed in The Guinness Book of World Records for the feat of pulling an 80-foot boat filled with passengers a distance of 300 feet while doing the backstroke — at the age of 69 and after having been diagnosed with cancer.

Jock Sutherland (March 21, 1889 — April 11, 1948)

Sutherland coached college football at Lafayette College and the University of Pittsburgh between 1919 and 1938, and coached professional football for the Brooklyn Dodgers and the Pittsburgh Steelers between 1940 and 1947. He was elected to the College Football Hall of Fame in 1951.

Walter Tewksbury (March 21, 1876 — April 24, 1968)

Track and field athlete Walter Tewksbury won five medals, including two gold, at the 1900 Summer Olympics.

John Tewksbury

Who Died on March 21?

Arts and Publishing

Wilbert Awdry (June 15, 1911 — March 21, 1997)

Cleric and railway enthusiast Reverend W. Audrey created *Thomas the Tank Engine.*

Thomas the Tank Engine

Cyril M. Kornbluth (July 2, 1923 — March 21, 1958)

Science fiction writer Kornbluth was an a member of the Futurian Society. His notable stories include "The Little Black Bag, " adapted for television twice, and "The Marching Morons." He is perhaps best remembered for his novel with Frederick Pohl, *The Space Merchants.*

Nadar (April 6, 1820 — March 21, 1910)

Gaspard-Félix Tournachon, known as Nadar, was an early photographer who also did caricatures, wrote novels, and built a balloon that inspired a Jules Verne's novel. He was the first person to take aerial photographs and pioneered the use of artificial lighting in photography. His work is part of many important photographic collections.

Drawing "Nadar: Elevating Photography to the Height of Art," by Honoré Daumier

Film and Television

Barney Martin (March 3, 1923 — March 21, 2005)

Martin was best known for playing Liza Minnelli's father in *Arthur* and Jerry Seinfeld's father in *Seinfeld*. He was an NYPD police officer for twenty years.

Ernie Wise (November 27, 1925 — March 21, 1999)

Wise was the semi-straight man half of the British comedy duo Morecambre and Wise, particularly known for their Christmas specials.

Dack Rambo (November 13, 1941 — March 21, 1994)

Rambo played Steve Jacobi in *All My Children*, Jack Ewing on *Dallas*, and Grant Harrison on *Another World*.

Lili Damita (July 10, 1904 — March 21, 1994)

Damita acted in silent fims and later appeared in the 1929 box office hits *The Cock-Eyed World* and *The Bridge of San Luis Rey*. She was married to Errol Flynn from 1935 to 1942.

Portrait of Lily Damita, 1929

Macdonald Carey (March 15, 1913 — March 21, 1994)

Carey played Dr. Tom Horton on *Days of Our Lives* for nearly 30 years.

John Ireland (January 30, 1914 — March 21, 1992)

Ireland is known for his many roles in Westerns including *My Darling Clementine* and *Red River*. He received an Oscar nomination for his role in 1949's *All the King's Men*.

Robert Preston (June 8, 1918 — March 21, 1987)

Preston is best remembered for originating the role of Harold Hill in *The Music Man* on Broadway and in film. He was nominated for an Oscar for his 1982 performance in *Victor Victoria*.

Dean Paul Martin (November 17, 1951 — March 21, 1987)

Dean Paul Martin, also known as Dino Martin Jr., was the son of actor and musician Dean Martin. As a teenager, he was a member of the pop rock group Dino, Desi, & Billy. He received a Golden Globe nomination for his 1979 film with Ali MacGraw, *Players*, and co-starred in the TV series *Misfits of Science*. A captain in the California Air National Guard, he died when his F-4 Phantom crashed during a snowstorm.

Dino, Desi, & Billy (left to right): Billy Hinsche, Desi Arnaz Jr., and **Dino Martin, Jr.**

Michael Redgrave (March 20, 1908 — March 21, 1985)

Michael Redgrave was best known as a theater actor in London, but received an Academy Award nomination for Best Actor for his role in 1947's *Mourning Becomoes Electra*. He was knighted in 1959.

His daughters Vanessa Redgrave and Lynn Redgrave and granddaughters Natashia and Joely Richardson are also well known actors.

Candy Darling (November 24, 1944 — March 21, 1974)

Candy Darling, a male-to-female transsexual born as James Slattery, starred in such Andy Warhol films as 1968's *Flesh* and 1971's *Women in Revolt* and was labeled as one of the Warhol "superstars."

Music and Dance

Pinetop Perkins (July 7, 1913 — March 21, 2011)

Blues pianist Joseph William Perkins (next page) received a Grammy Lifetime Achievement Award and was inducted into the Blues Hall of Fame.

Bobby Short (September 15, 1924 — March 21, 2005)

Cabaret singer and pianist Bobby Short was a featured performer at the Café Carlyle in New York for over 35 years, and became more widely known for performing in a commercial for the Revlon perfume "Charlie." He appeared in the Woody Allen film *Hannah and Her Sister* and his recording of "I Happen to Like New York" opened *Manhattan Murder Mystery*. He was named a Living Legend by the Library of Congress in 2000.

Pinetop Perkins

Ludmilla Tchérina (October 10, 1924 — March 21, 2004)

In her 1942 Paris debut, Tchérina became the youngest prima ballerina in the history of dance. She appeared in several films, including *The Red Shoes*. In addition, she wrote two novels, and her painting and sculpture has been exhibited in numerous galleries.

Galina Ulanova (Галина Уланова) (January 8 [O.S. December 26], 1909 — March 21, 1998)

One of the greatest ballerinas of the 20th century, Galina Ulanova was named People's Artist of the USSR, its highest artistic honor. Her apartment in Moscow is preserved as a museum. Composer Sergey Prokofiev said of her, "She is the genius of Russian ballet, its elusive soul, its inspired poetry."

Leo Fender (August 20, 1909 — March 21, 1991)

Inventor Leo Fender designed and built iconic electric guitars including the Fender Telecaster and the Fender Stratocaster. He is in the Rock and Roll Hall of Fame.

Louis Cottrell, Jr. (March 7, 1911 — March 21, 1978)

Creole clarinet and tenor sax player Louis Cottrell Jr., led the Heritage Hall Jazz Band at its famous 1974 Carnegie Hall Concert. His father and his grandson were also noted jazz musicians.

Politics and Military

Herman Talmadge (August 9, 1913 — March 21, 2002)

As governor of Georgia from 1947 to 1955 and senator from 1957 to 1981, Talmadge was known for his segregationist politics.

Arthur Nebe (November 13, 1894 — March 21, 1945)

Nazi Arthur Nebe commanded early Holocaust units (Einsatzgruppe), and as President of Interpol. He joined the failed 1944 bomb plot against Adolf Hitler, but was betrayed by an ex-mistress, convicted of treason, and killed."

Cornelia Fort (February 5, 1919 — March 21, 1943)

Cornelia Fort was the first female pilot in American history to die on active duty.

She was teaching student pilots on December 7, 1941, when she became one of the first witnesses of the Japanese attack on Pearl Harbor, and managed to land safely with a Japanese Zero fighter on her tail.

She died ferrying planes when a male pilot crashed into her in a mid-air collision.

Cornelia Fort

General Edwin V. Sumner (January 30, 1797 — March 21, 1863)

Union officer Edwin "Bull Head" Sumner was the oldest field commander on either side during the American Civil War. He led II Corps of the Army of the Potomac through the Peninsula Campaign, the Maryland Campaign, and the Battle of Fredericksburg.

Guadalupe Victoria (September 29, 1786 — March 21, 1843)

Victoria was the first president of Mexico, serving from 1824 to 1829.

John Law (baptized April 21, 1671 — March 21, 1729)

Scottish economist John Law established the first French central bank, which was responsible for the Mississippi Bubble and the resultant economic collapse in France. He fled the country disguised as a woman, spent the next years as a gambler, and died a poor man.

Public Figures

Kevin Whitrick (August 17, 1964 — March 21, 2007)

British engineer Whitrick committed suicide by hanging himself online during a webcast chat.

Chung Ju-yung (정주영) (November 25, 1915 — March 21, 2001)

Korean entrepreneur Ju-yung founded the Hyundai Group.

Angelo Bruno (May 21, 1910 — March 21, 1980)

Sicilian-American mobster Angelo Bruno was known as the "Gentle Don" during his long reign as head of the Philadelphia crime family.

Joe "Ducky" Medwick (November 24, 1911 — March 21, 1975)

Medwick was an American League left fielder for the St. Louis Cardinals during the "Gashouse Gang" era, and later played for the Dodgers, the Giants, and the Braves. He was inducted into the Baseball Hall of Fame in 1968.

Frederick W. Taylor (March 20, 1856 — March 21, 1915)

Frederick Winslow Taylor began his career as an engineer, but turned his attention to industrial efficiency. He is known as the "father of scientific management" and as one of the first management consultants.

James Ussher (January 4, 1581 — March 21, 1656)

Irish archbishop James Ussher is best known for his chronology of Biblical events that claimed to establish the exact day of creation as Sunday, October 23, 4004 BCE.

Archbishop James Ussher by Peter Lely

Pocahontas (c. 1595 — buried March 21, 1617)

Daughter of Powhatan, a Native-American chief in Virginia, Pocahontas (right) is said to have saved the life of John Smith, an Englishman from the Jamestown settlement by placing her head on his when her  father was about to execute him.

She was captured by the English and held for ransom, and rather than return home, she stayed with the English and married tobacco farmer John Rolfe in the first recorded interracial marriage in American history.

She died on a trip to London, survived by her husband and her son Thomas Rolfe. Her notable descendants through her son include Nancy Reagan and astronomer Percival Lowell.

Her story has been largely mythologized and retold in a number of films, including the 1995 Disney animated feature *Pocahontas*.

Science

Peter Stoner (June 16, 1888 — March 21, 1980)

Science professor and department head Peter Stoner is known for his book of relating science to the Bible, *Science Speaks*.

Giovanni Arduino (October 16, 1714 — March 21, 1795)

Known as the "father of Italian geology," Arduino developed the first classification of geological time: primitive, secondary, tertiary and quarternary, some of which is still used today.

Nicolas Louis de Lacaille (May 15, 1713 — March 21, 1762)

French astronomer de Lacaille compiled the first comprehensive catalog of the stars of the Southern Hemisphere, introducing 14 new constellations, and calculated future eclipses for the next 1,800 years.

The month of March, from the illuminated manuscript *Les Très Riches Heures du duc de Berry*

March: The Third Month

"Up from the sea, the wild north wind is blowing
Under the sky's gray arch;
Smiling I watch the shaken elm boughs, knowing
It is the wind of March."

                    — *"March," John Greenleaf Whittier*

In ancient Rome, March was the first month of the year. As the first month of spring, in the Mediterranean climate it marked the beginning of the military campaign season. That's why March (Martius) is named in honor of Mars, the Roman god of war.

Although the first month of the year was moved back to January sometime during the transition of Rome from a kingdom to a republic (historians differ), March was the first month of the year in Russia until the end of the 15th Century, and is the first month of the year in many other cultures and religions.

In the northern hemisphere, March 1 marks the beginning of meteorological spring. In the southern hemisphere, March is the equivalent of September, making southern hemisphere March the beginning of autumn.

March is one of the seven months that have 31 days in it. March starts on the same day of the week as November every year, and except for leap years starts on the same day as February. March starts on the same day of the week as the previous June except for leap years, and in leap years starts on the same day as the previous September and December.

March in Other Cultures

In Finland, March is called *maaliskuu* (earthy month). In Ukraine, it's *березень* (birch tree). Other names for March include *Lentmonat* (Saxon), *Hyld-monath* (Angles), and *sušec* (Slovene).

March Symbols

Birthstones: Aquamarine (left) and bloodstone, both representing courage.

Birth Flowers: Daffodils

Daffodils in Bagatelle Park, Paris, France

March Events

Honorary months: Presidents, Congresses, and nations around the world issue proclamations recognizing particular months to honor certain causes. The following events generally fall in March. (All US unless noted.)

- National Nutrition Month
- American Red Cross Month
- Women's History Month (U.S.)

- Irish-American Heritage Month
- Colorectal Cancer Awareness Month
- Fire Prevention Month (The Philippines)

"March Madness": (United States) The NCAA Men's Division I Basketball Championship, popularly known as "March Madness" or the "Big Dance," is a single-elimination tournament to establish the champion college basketball team.

Multi-day events: Some March events span multiple days.

* **Multiple Sclerosis Awareness Week:** (U.S.) Sponsored by the National Multiple Sclerosis Society, MS Awareness Week is normally held on the second full week in March. The earliest it can begin is March 9 and the latest end is March 21.

Movable events: Some events change dates from year to year.

* **March Equinox:** As the Earth's axis tilts toward and away from the sun during the year, it reaches two extremes, known as the *solstices,* and two times in which the tilt is in the middle) neither toward nor away from the sun), known as the *equinoxes.* At the equinox, the length of the day and the length of the night are approximately equal.

    The *vernal,* or spring, equinox is the official beginning of springtime. The *autumnal,* or fall, equinox is the official beginning of fall. The March Equinox, which falls between March 19 and March 21, depending on the year, is the *vernal equinox* in the Northern Hemisphere, and the *autumnal equinox* in the Southern Hemisphere.

- **Earth Day:** Earth Day, an international day to increase awareness and appreciation of our planet's natural environment, is held each year on the same day as the March equinox, between March 19 and March 21.

    The first Earth Day took place in 1970, and there are now Earth Day events held in over 140 nations around the world. Some communities celebrate Earth Week, which is the week containing Earth Day.

- **Nowruz:** New Year's Day in Iran is known as Nowruz, and it takes place on the same day as the March equinox, between March 19 and March 21. Nowruz is also a holiday in Turkey and some Central Asian countries, and is celebrated wherever large concentrations of Iranians live.

    It was originally a holiday of the Zoroastrian religion, and the Islamic rulers of Iran have attempted to suppress it, though with little success. Nowruz is also a holy day for Alawites, Alevis, and Bahá'í. Fire is the symbol of Nowruz, and large bonfires often play a part in festivities.

Zoroastrian bas-relief of Nowruz. The bull (representing Earth) and the lion (the Sun) are equal, a symbol of the equinox

- **New Age/Neopagan Events:** Numerous occult, Wiccan, and neopagan groups celebrate the equinox. It is *Thelemic New Year* and *Ostara* (Northern Hemisphere) or *Mabon* (Southern Hemisphere) in Wicca. It is also International Astrology Day.

- **Shunbun no Hi** (春分の日)**:** In Japan, Vernal Equinox Day is a national holiday for the admiration of nature and the love of living things.

- **World Storytelling Day:** On World Storytelling Day, people tell and hear stories in as many languages and places as possible during the same day and night. The event began in Sweden and expanded worldwide.

Easter Events

La crucifixión by El Greco

The Easter Season

The Christian holiday of Easter in Western Christianity is held on the first Sunday after the Paschal Full Moon following the March equinox, which is officially set at March 21 by church reckoning. Easter itself can therefore occur as early as March 22 and as late as April 25, but occurs most often in April.

In Eastern Christianity, which uses the Julian calendar, Easter occurs between April 4 and May 8. This also sets the date for the various events that lead up to Easter, especially Holy Week.

The following events can sometimes takes place on March 21.

Passion Sunday

The fifth Sunday of the Christian season of Lent is known as Passion Sunday in various Protestant denominations and by some traditionalist Catholics.

Passion Sunday starts the two-week Passiontide, which ends on Holy Saturday, the day before Easter, commemorating the day that Jesus's body was laid in the tomb. The fifth Sunday of Lent can occur as early as March 8 (though the next time it will be that early is in 2285 CE), and as late as April 11.

Palm Sunday

Palm Sunday commemorates the triumphant entry of Jesus into Jerusalem, an event mentioned in all four gospels. In many Christian churches, palm leaves are distributed to the worshippers. The earliest date for Palm Sunday is March 15, and the latest is April 18.

Maundy Thursday

The Thursday before Easter is Maundy Thursday, when the Last Supper took place. The earliest can occur is March 19, and the latest it can occur is April 22.

Good Friday

Good Friday, observed during Holy Week on the Friday preceding Easter Sunday, commemorates the crucifixion of Jesus and his death at Calvary. Because of its relation to Easter, the earliest day it can occur is March 20, and the latest it can occur is April 23.

Holy Saturday

Sometimes called Easter Eve or Black Saturday, Holy Saturday commemorates the day in which Jesus's body lay in the tomb. Some mistakenly refer to this day as "Easter Saturday," but that is the Saturday *following* Easter, the last day of Easter Week. The earliest it can occur is March 21, and the latest it can occur is April 24.

March Zodiac Signs

From the perspective of someone on Earth, the Sun appears to move through the sky throughout the year, along a path astronomers call the ecliptic plane. The ecliptic plane is divided into twelve constellations, known as the zodiac, based on traditionally observed patterns of stars. On your birthday, you can't see your constellation, because it's part of the daytime sky.

The zodiac was first developed by Babylonian astronomers about 2,500 years ago. Because they were unaware that the Earth wobbles like a spinning top (a motion known as *precession*), they didn't make allowance for the fact that the Sun's path through the zodiac changes over time.

That means there are now two sets of dates for your birth sign. The *tropical* dates are the original Babylonian dates; the *siderial* dates tell you where the Sun actually appears as it moves along its annual path.

In siderial reckoning, March 21 is in Pisces, but in tropical astrology, March 21 is the first day of Aries. (In some calculations, the transition between Pisces and Aries is related to the first day of the March equinox, meaning that March 20 in some years is the first day of tropical Aries.)

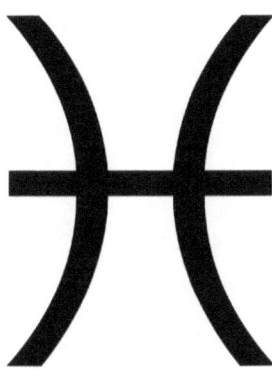

Pisces

Tropical February 20 to March 20

Siderial March 15 to April 14

In the Roman legend of Venus and her son Cupid, they escaped the clutches of Typhon, known as the "father of all monsters," by transforming into fish and tying themselves together with rope. That's why the name Pisces is plural for fish. The constellation appears as a somewhat ragged "V" shape, representing the rope, with the "fish" located at the two rope ends.

In astrology, Pisces is a water sign, compatible with the other water signs Cancer and Scorpio, as well as with the earth signs Taurus, Virgo, and Capricorn. Pisceans are supposed to be imaginative, compassionate, unworldly, secretive, and escapist.

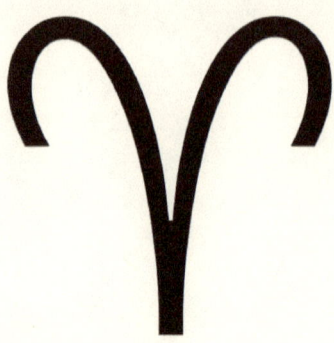

Aries

Tropical March 21 to April 19

Siderial April 15 to May 15

In Greek mythology, Aries is a ram with golden wings and golden wool who rescued the twins Phrixus and Helle from certain death. Although Helle died in the rescue attempt, the grateful Phrixus sacrificed the ram to Zeus. The golden fleece from the sacrificed ram played a prominent part in the later myth of Jason and the Argonauts.

In astrology, Aries, a fire sign, is compatible with the other fire signs of Gemini, Leo, and Sagittarius, and to a lesser extent with air signs Scorpio and Libra. Arians are   supposed to adventurous, enthusiastic, quick-tempered, and impulsive.

What Day of the Week is March 21?

On what day of the week does March 21 fall?

Surprisingly, this isn't an easy question. Because the calendar year is 365 days long (366 in leap years), it doesn't divide evenly by the seven days of the week.

Also, the Earth goes around the Sun in about 365-1/4 days, so a calendar tends to drift over time. That's why the same date falls on different weekdays in different years.

This is made even more complicated by a change in calendars that took place in 1582. Our modern calendar has its roots in ancient Rome, in a calendar reform conducted by Julius Caesar. Caesar commissioned mathematicians to attack the problem, and came up with the idea of *leap years,* and thus standardized the calendar for centuries to come. This was called the *Julian calendar.*

Over time, however, the small errors in Caesar's calculation compounded. That's why Pope Gregory XIII commissioned the *Gregorian calendar,* used in most of the world today. Some countries converted in 1582, when the calendar was first developed; some converted later; other still haven't changed.

Gregorian and Julian aren't the only types of calendars. The Hebrew year, the Islamic year, and many other calendars are used in different parts of the world and among different people.

You can convert Gregorian dates to other calendars, including the Hebrew calendar, the Islamic calendar, and even the Mayan calendar by visiting the Fourmilab Calendar Converter at http://www.fourmilab.ch/documents/calendar/.

A 50-year brass perpetual calendar.

Copyright, Credit, and Contact

Follow Us

Our blog Dobson's Improbable History features short articles on events and people associated with each day, and updates several times each week. Get the latest on Twitter @SidewiseThinker.

Contact Us

Find an error or a format problem? Want information about the series, about us, or about when the volume for your special day might be available? Please email us at editor@timespinnerpress.com.

Sources and Art Credits

All art and photographs are either in the public domain or used under a Creative Commons license. Attribution is provided where requested by the copyright owner or when of historical significance, listed below. Most images are from Wikimedia Commons.

- The 1965 film poster for Russ Meyer's *Faster, Pussycat! Kill! Kill!* is in the public domain because it was published between 1923 and 1977 without a copyright notice.

- The 1881 painting of Modest Mussorgsky by Ilya Repin is in the public domain because its copyright has expired.

- The painting of Saint Nicholas of Flüe (Brother Klaus) is in the public domain because its copyright has expired. The artist and date is unknown.

- The photograph of John Tewksbury is in the public domain because its copyright has expired.

- The photograph of Thomas the Tank Engine at Drusillas Zoo Park was taken by "Milborne One," and is used under the Creative Commons Attribution-Share Alike 3.0 Unported license. Thomas the Tank Engine is a trademark of HiT Entertainment._http://commons.wikimedia.org/wiki/File:Drusillas-006.jpg

- The drawing "Nadar, élevant la photographie à la hauteur de l'Art" by Honoré Daumier is in the public domain because its copyright has expired. The original drawing is in the collection of the Brooklyn Museum.

- The portrait of Lili Damita on the cover of the Argentine magazine *Cinelandia*, May 1929 issue, is in the public domain because its Argentinian copyright has expired.

- The 1965 photograph of Dino, Desi, & Billy is in the public domain because it was first published between 1923 and 197 without a copyright notice.

- The 2008 photograph of Pinetop Perkins was taken by "Cathy from Reno" at the Santa Cruz Blues Festival. It is used here under the Creative Commons Attribution 2.0 Generic license. http://commons.wikimedia.org/wiki/File:Pinetop_Perkins.jpg

- The photograph of aviator Cornelia Fort is in the public domain as a work of the U.S. federal government.

- The painting of Archbishop James Ussher by Peter Lely is in the public domain because its copyright has expired.

**Timespinner
Press**

www.ingramcontent.com/pod-product-compliance
Lightning Source LLC
Chambersburg PA
CBHW050430290526
45786CB00003B/1465